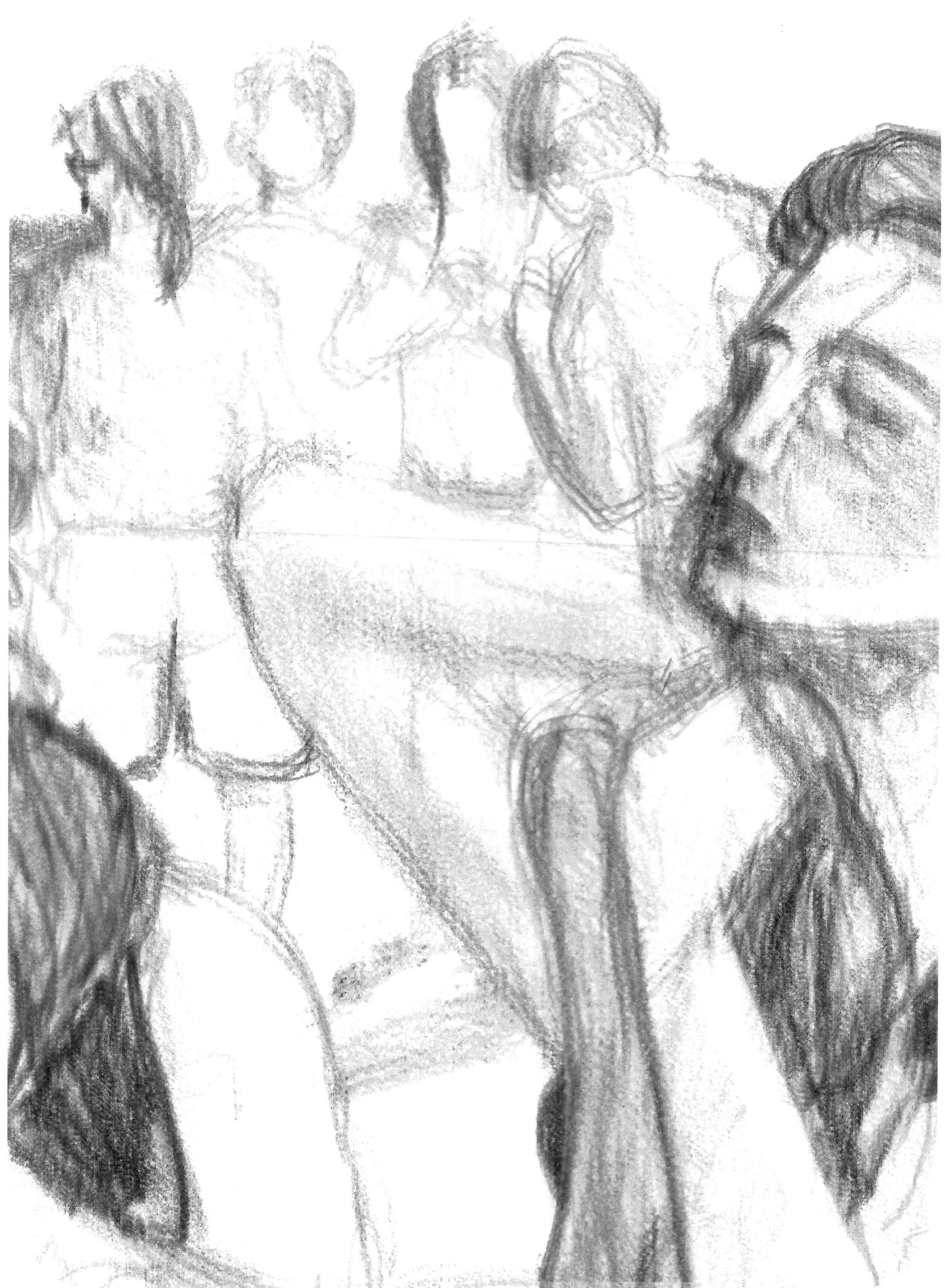

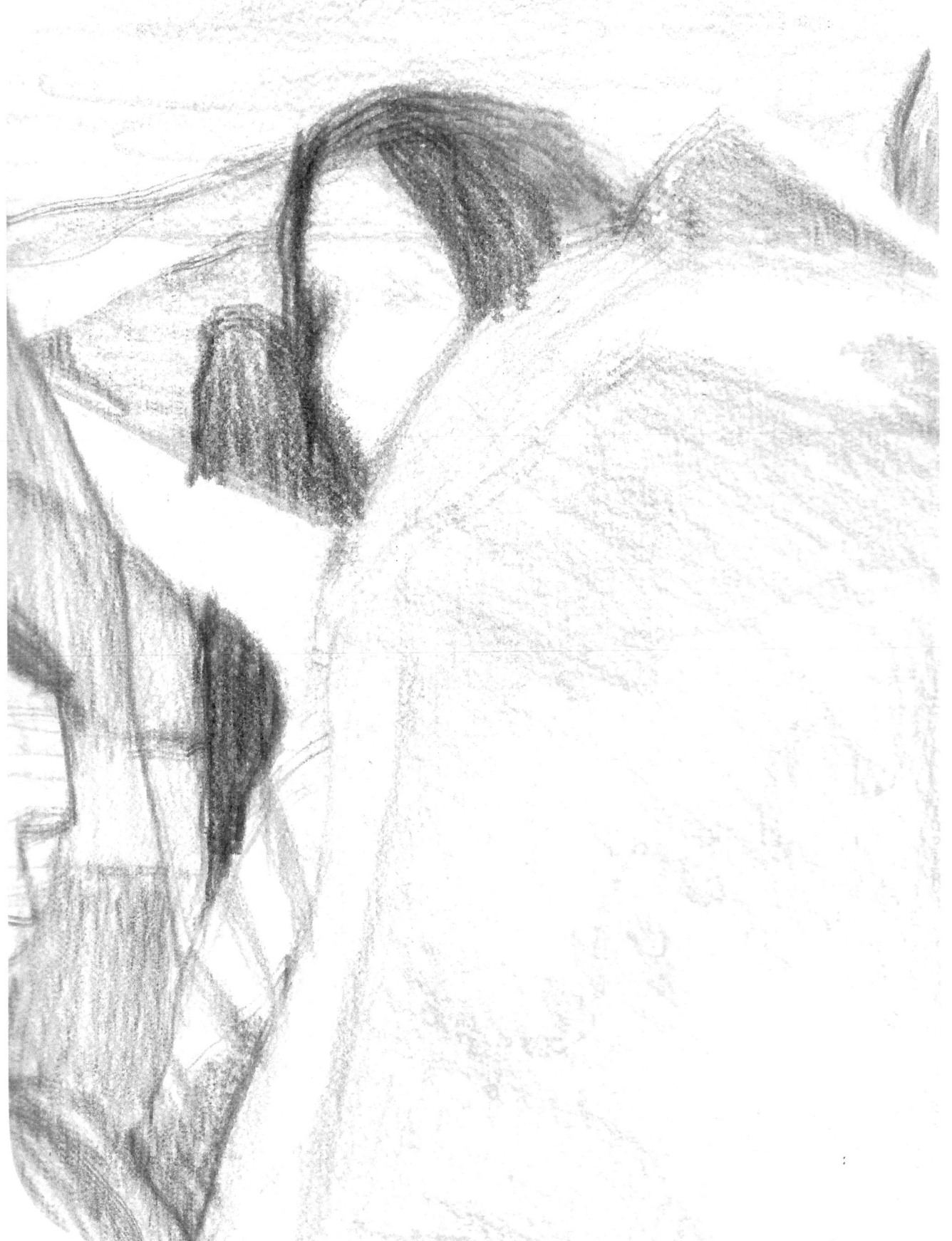

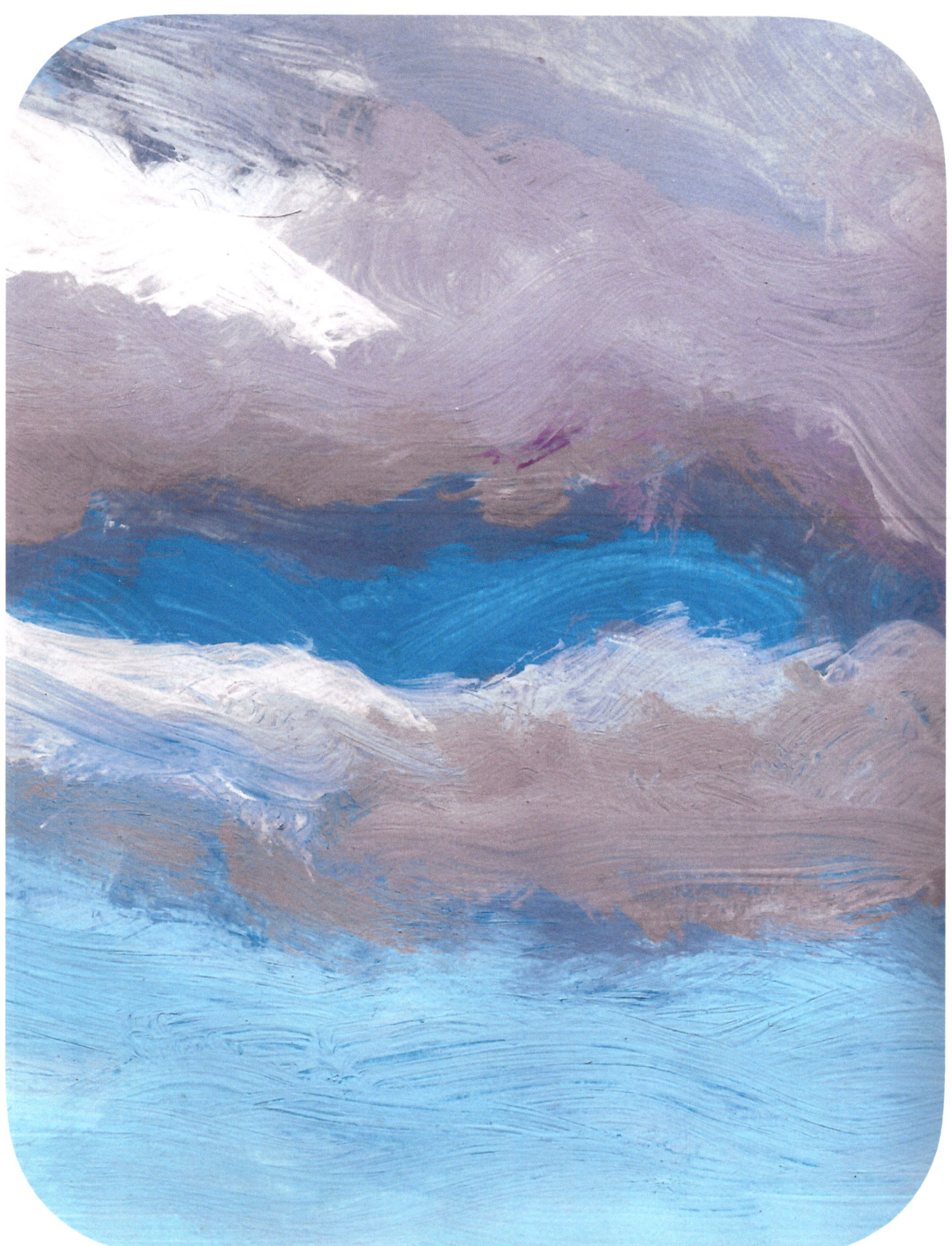

The Day of the Swim

By Andrew Dylan Campbell

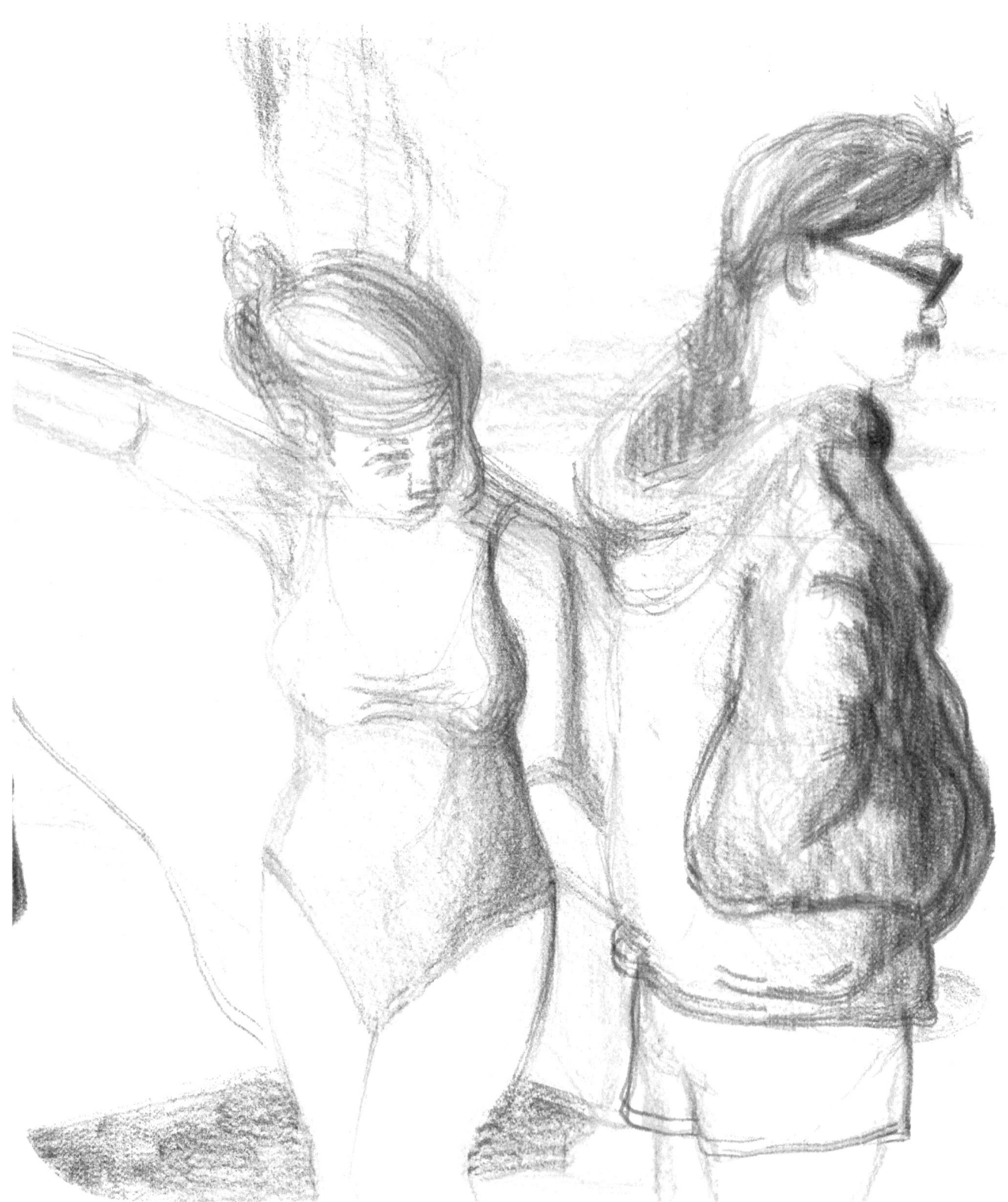

Every winter, on the day of the swim, everybody in town gathers on the beach. We all wear swimsuits and bring towels, even though it's cold.

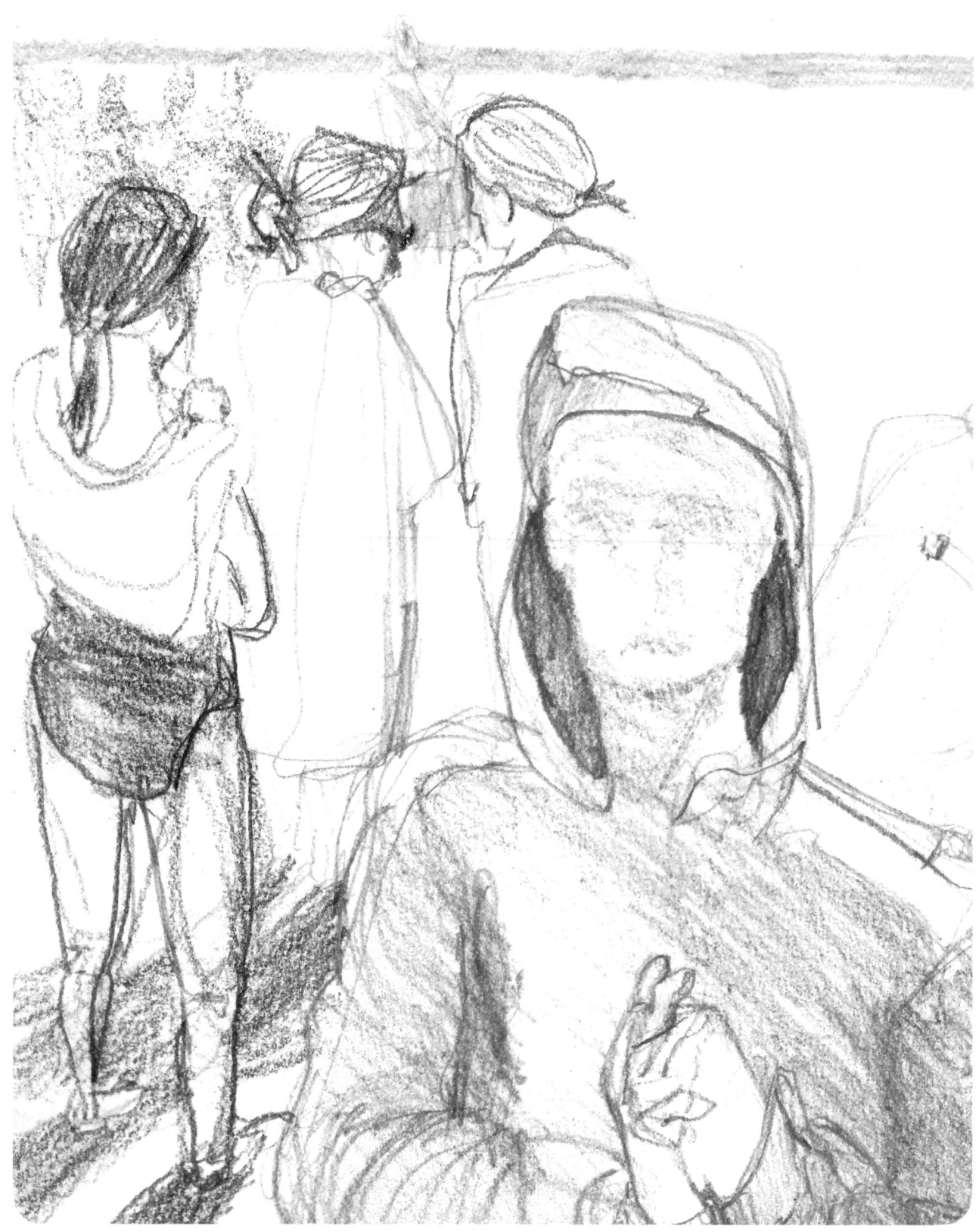

I don't like the cold, so I don't go in the water. But every year I come out to watch everyone take the plunge. Maybe I'll jump in this year. I don't know.

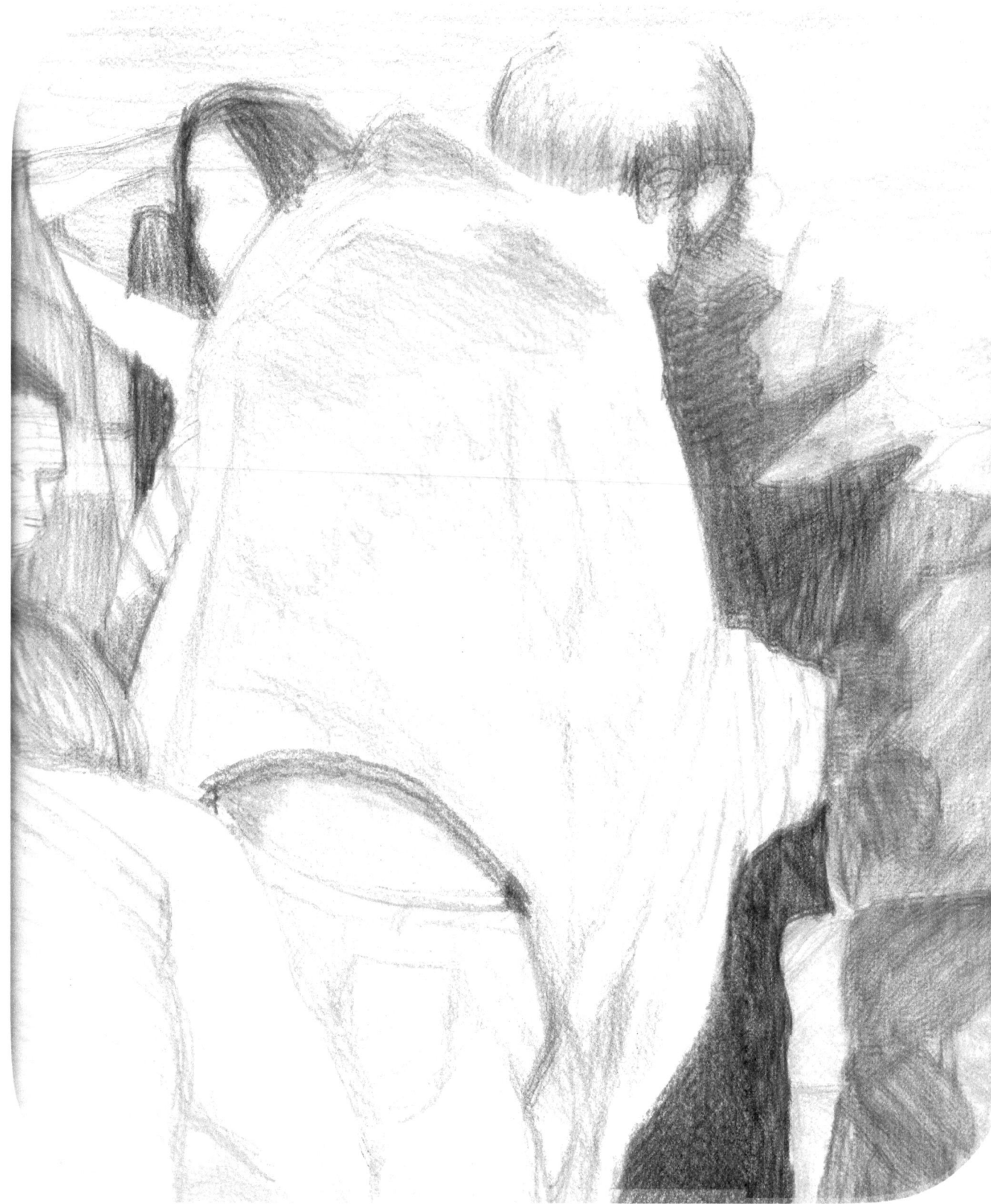

All of the people in town prepare for the swim in different ways. They share stories about their first time. I come to see the people. The crowds are very interesting.

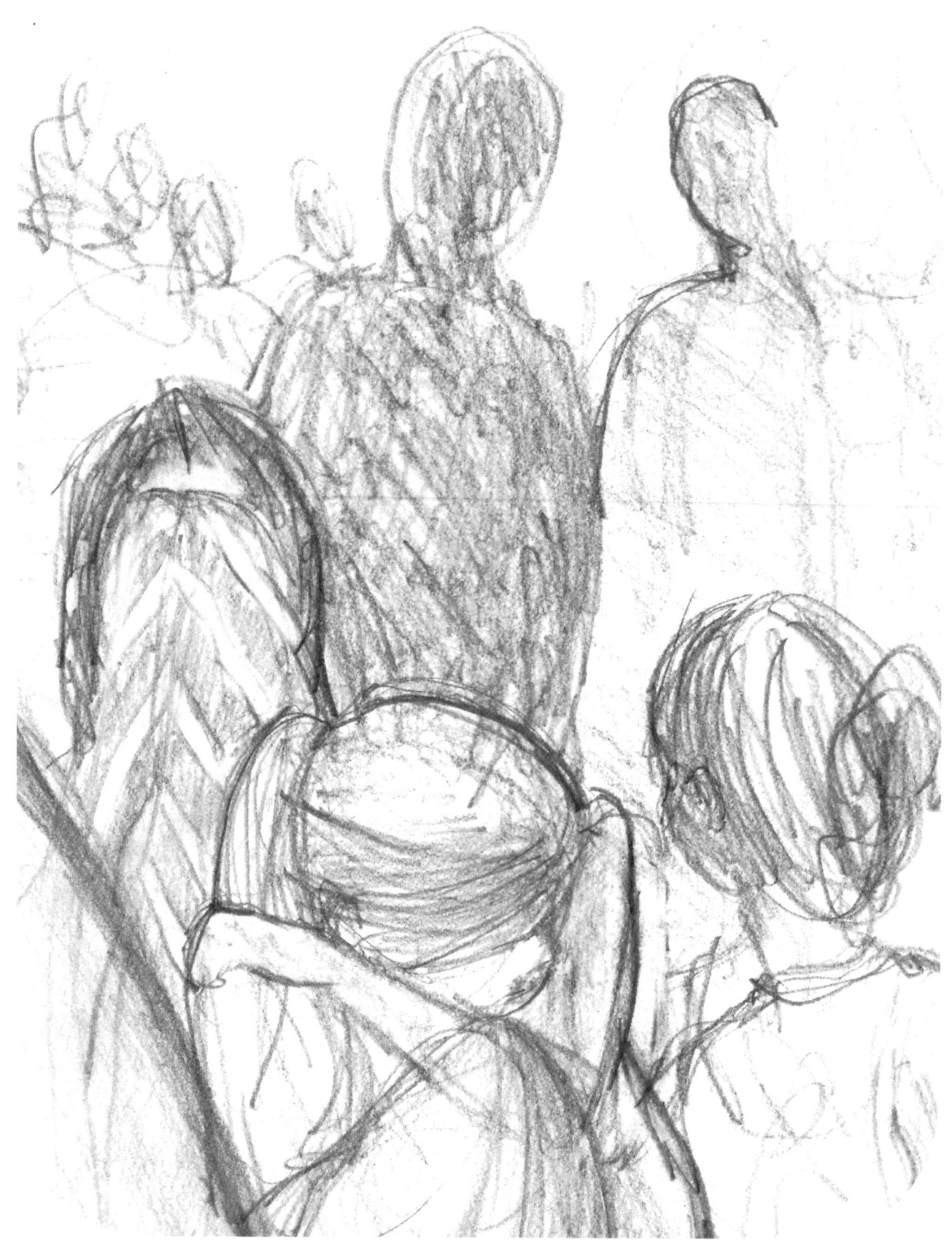

I don't take a towel with me on the day of the swim. I bring my sketchbook and pencil. I try to capture the energy of the crowds; it's relaxing.

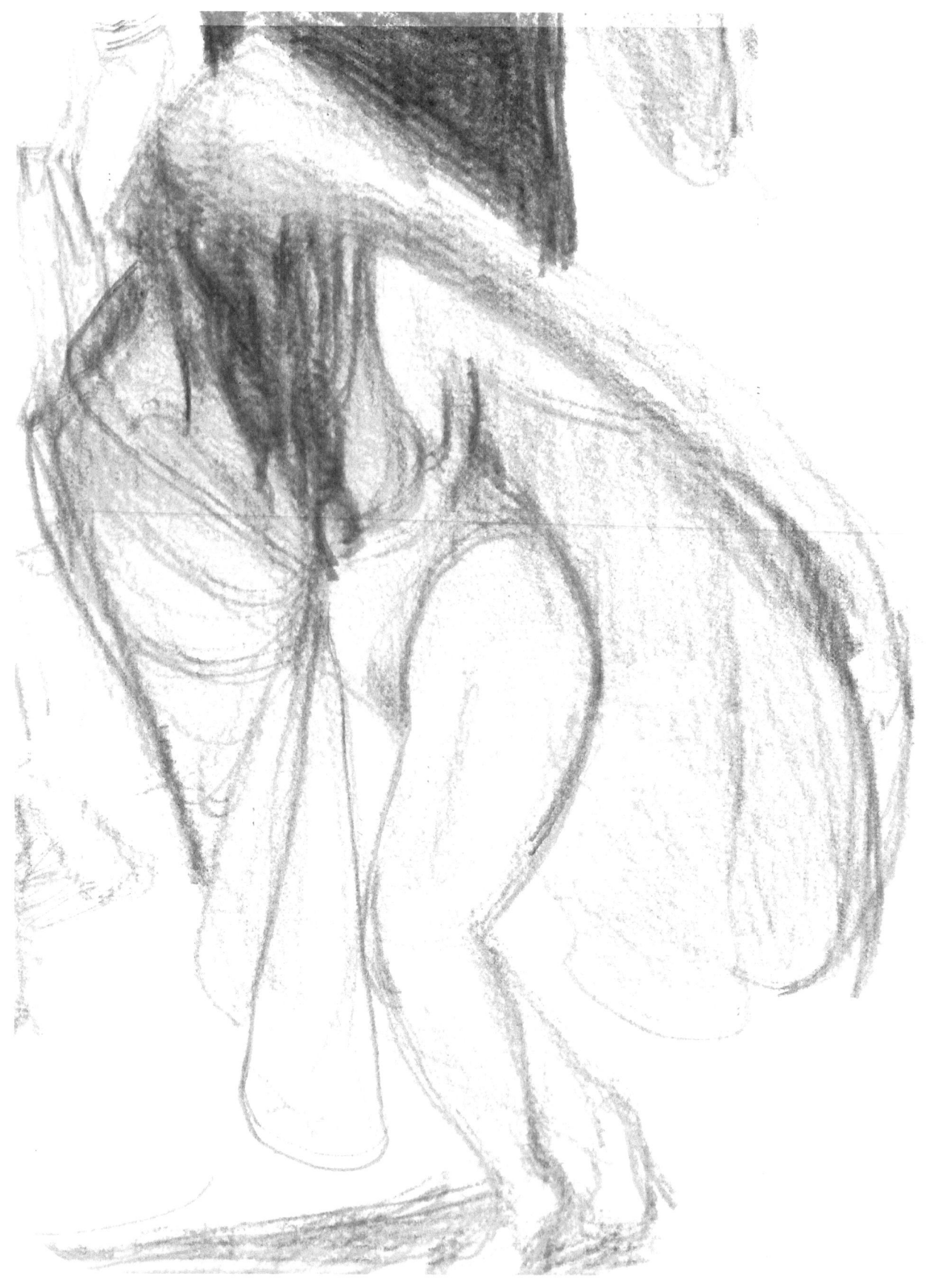

As the people move around me, I draw them quickly. If they stop and pose I draw what I see behind them. As I said, I'm interested in the crowds.

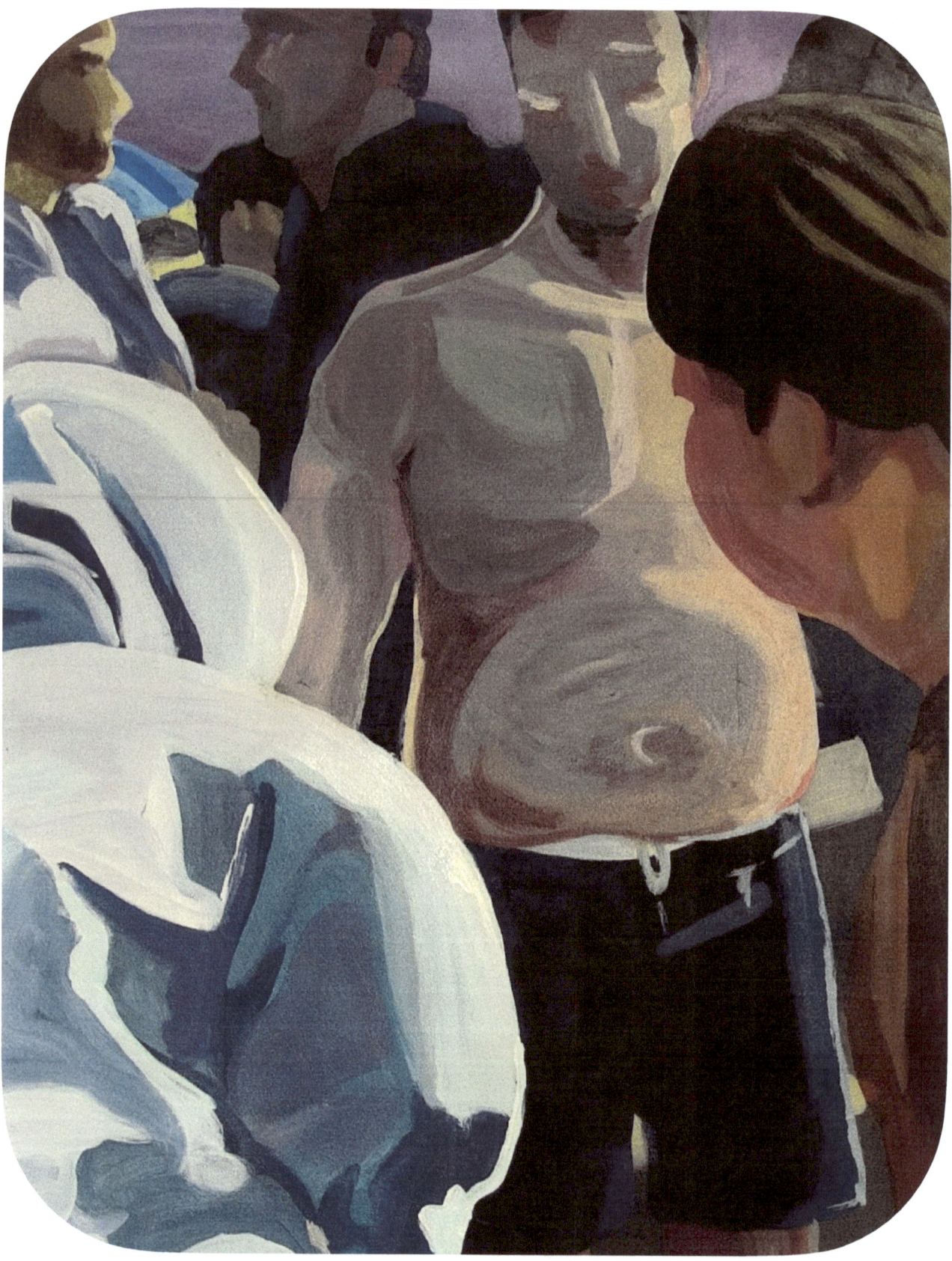

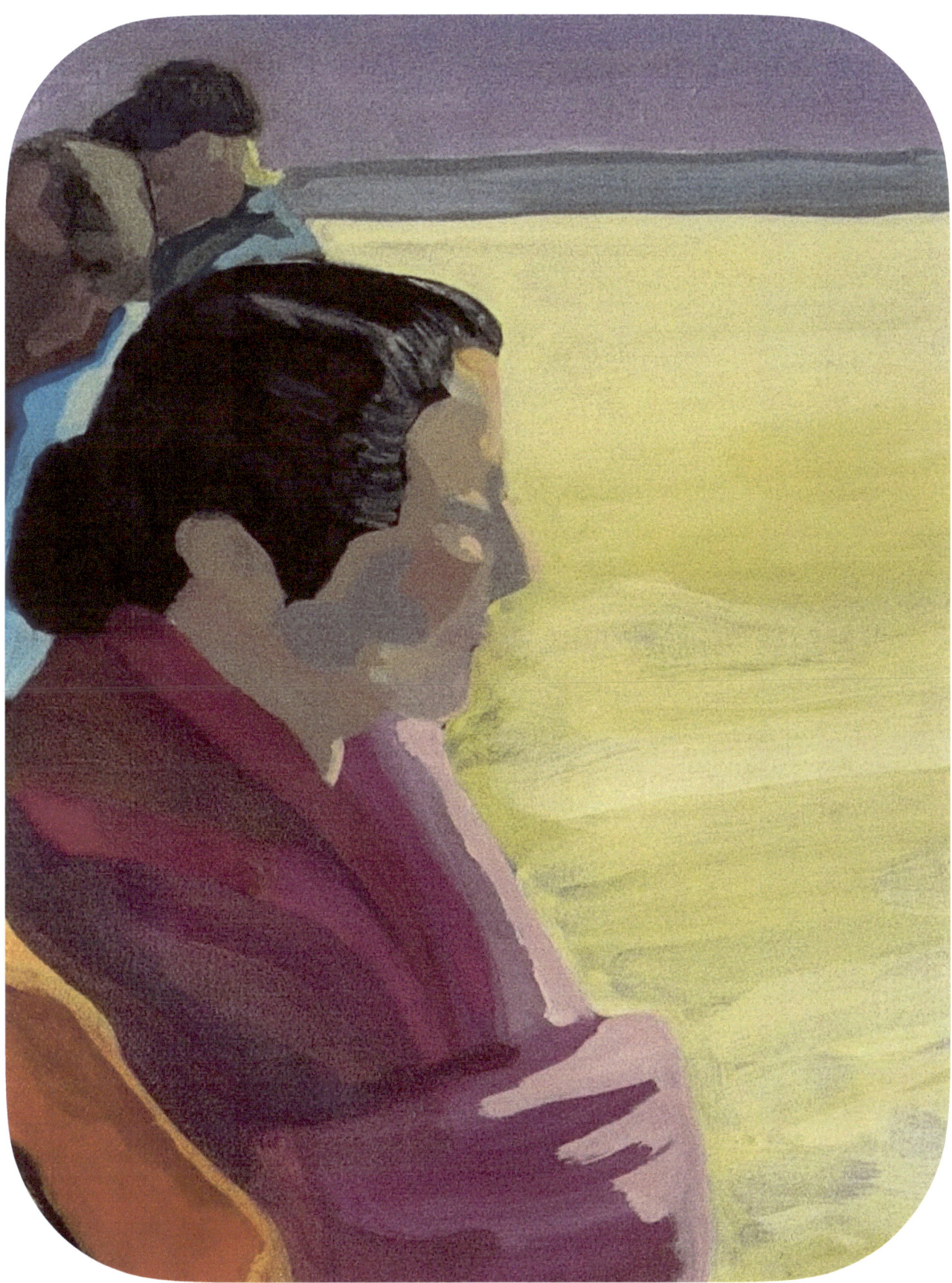

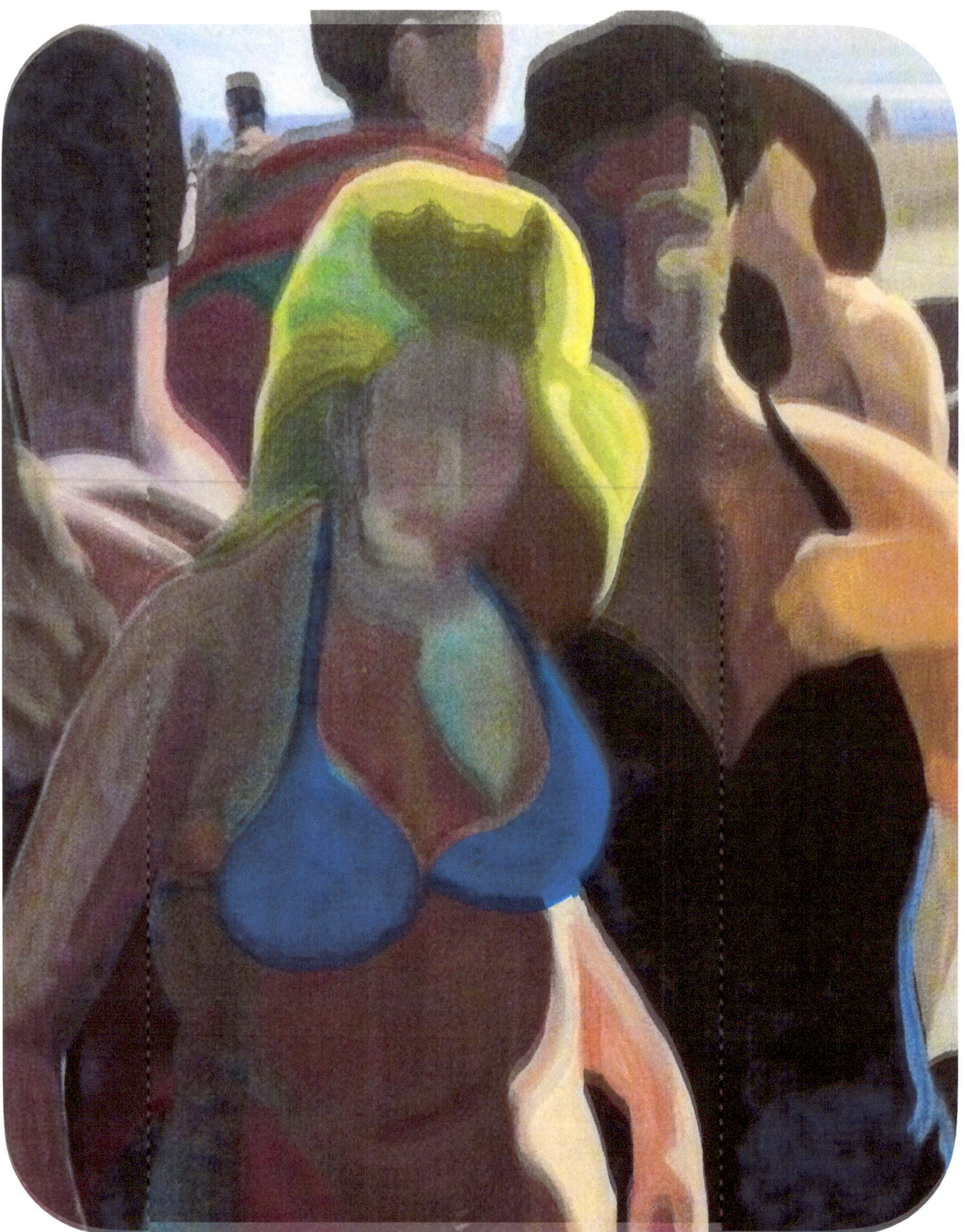

The noise of the crowd fills the air; it helps me focus. As all of the stories and cheers combine it is easier to forget about them.

When I am really focused, I start to see the colors and shapes that make up the crowd.

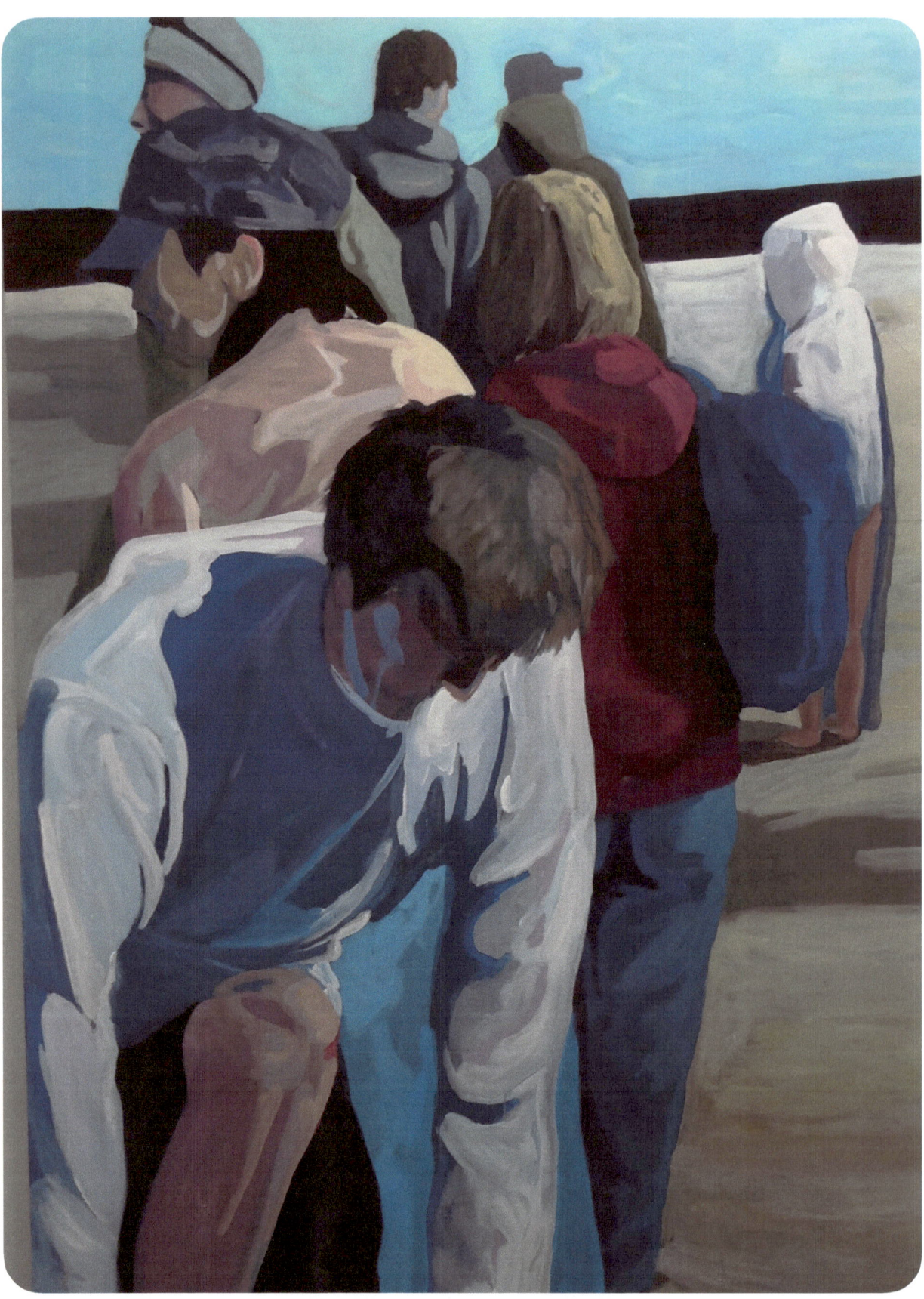

I begin to draw small groups of swimmers as they emerge from the cold water, eager to get dry and clothed once more.

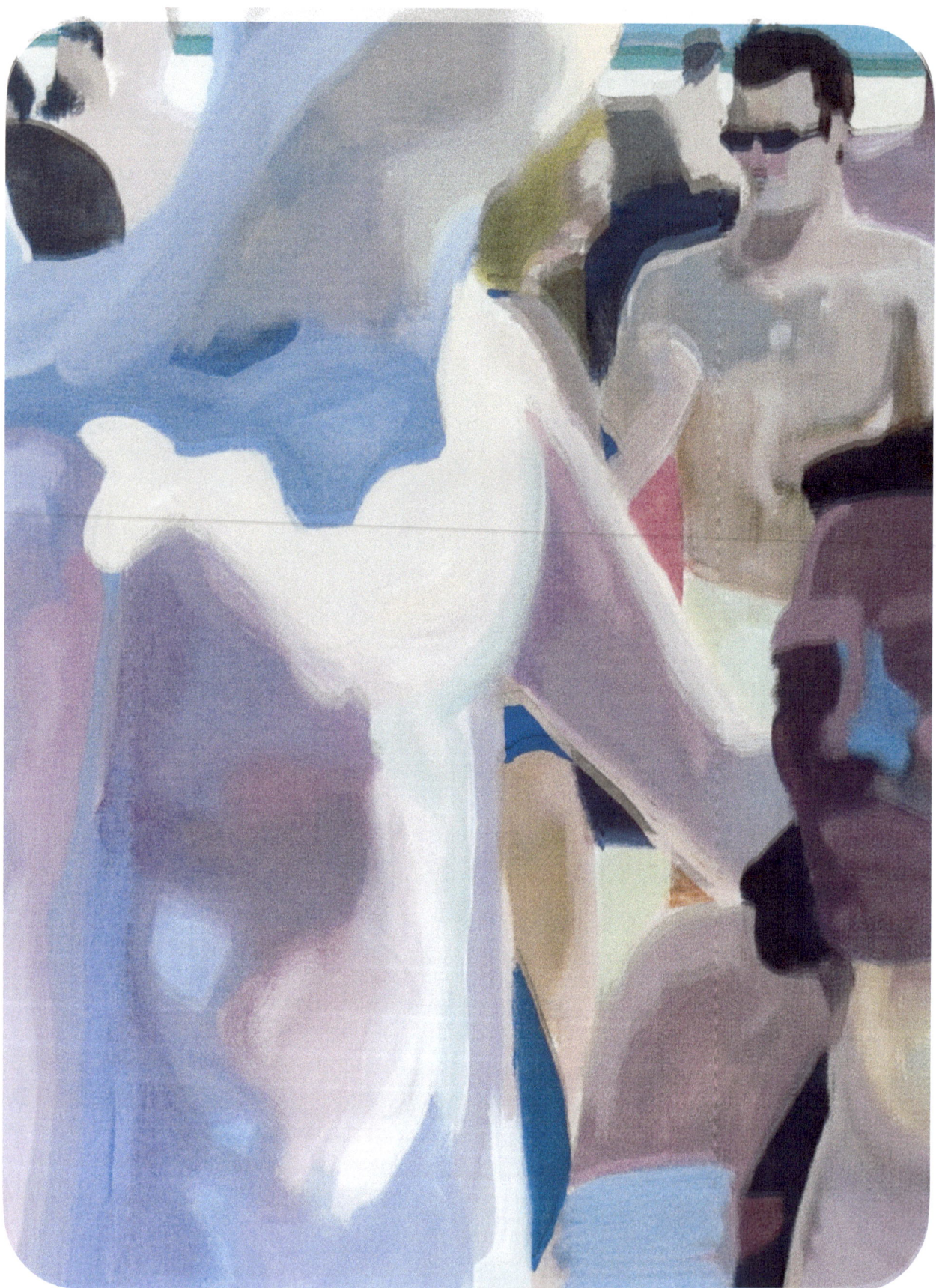

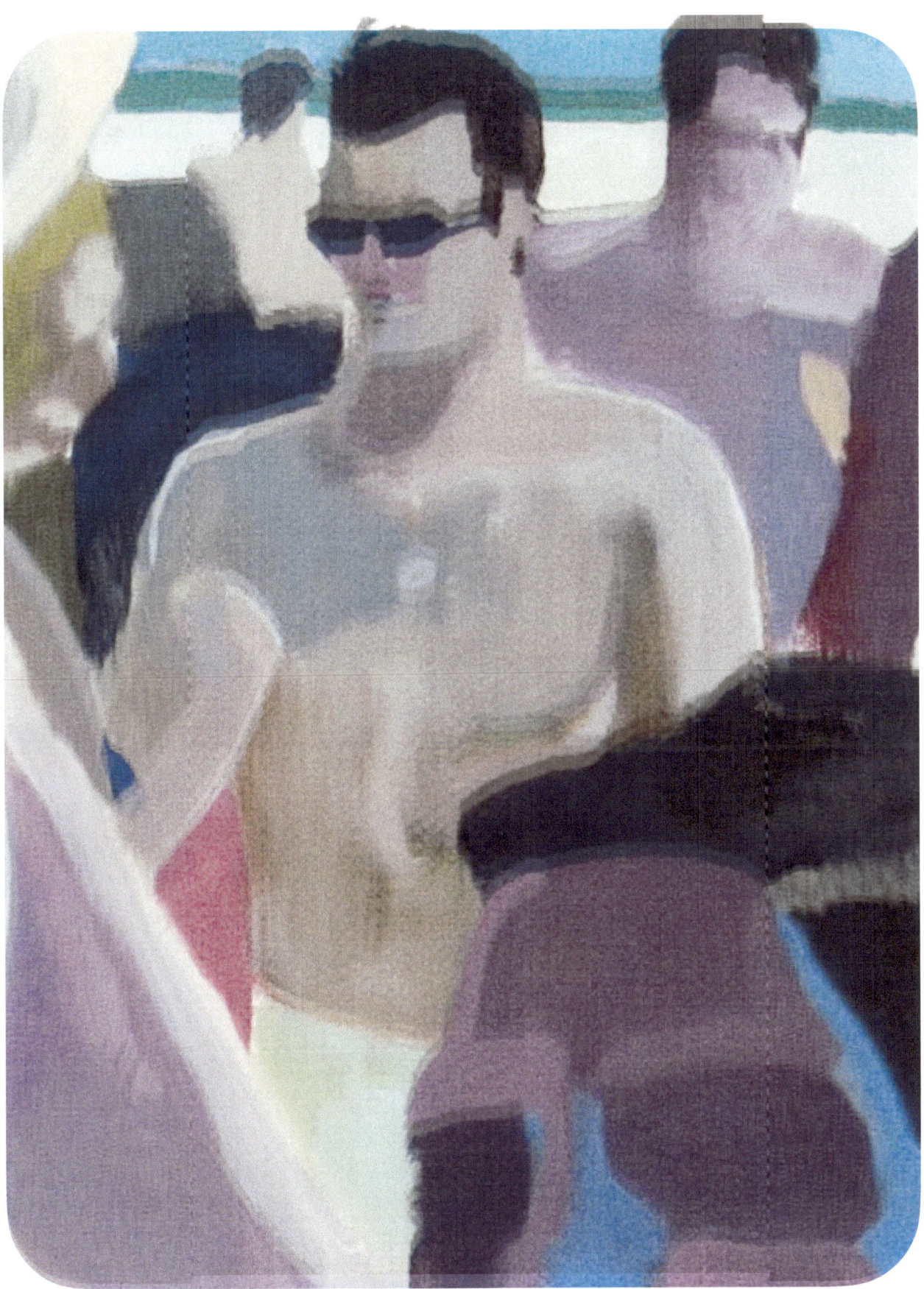

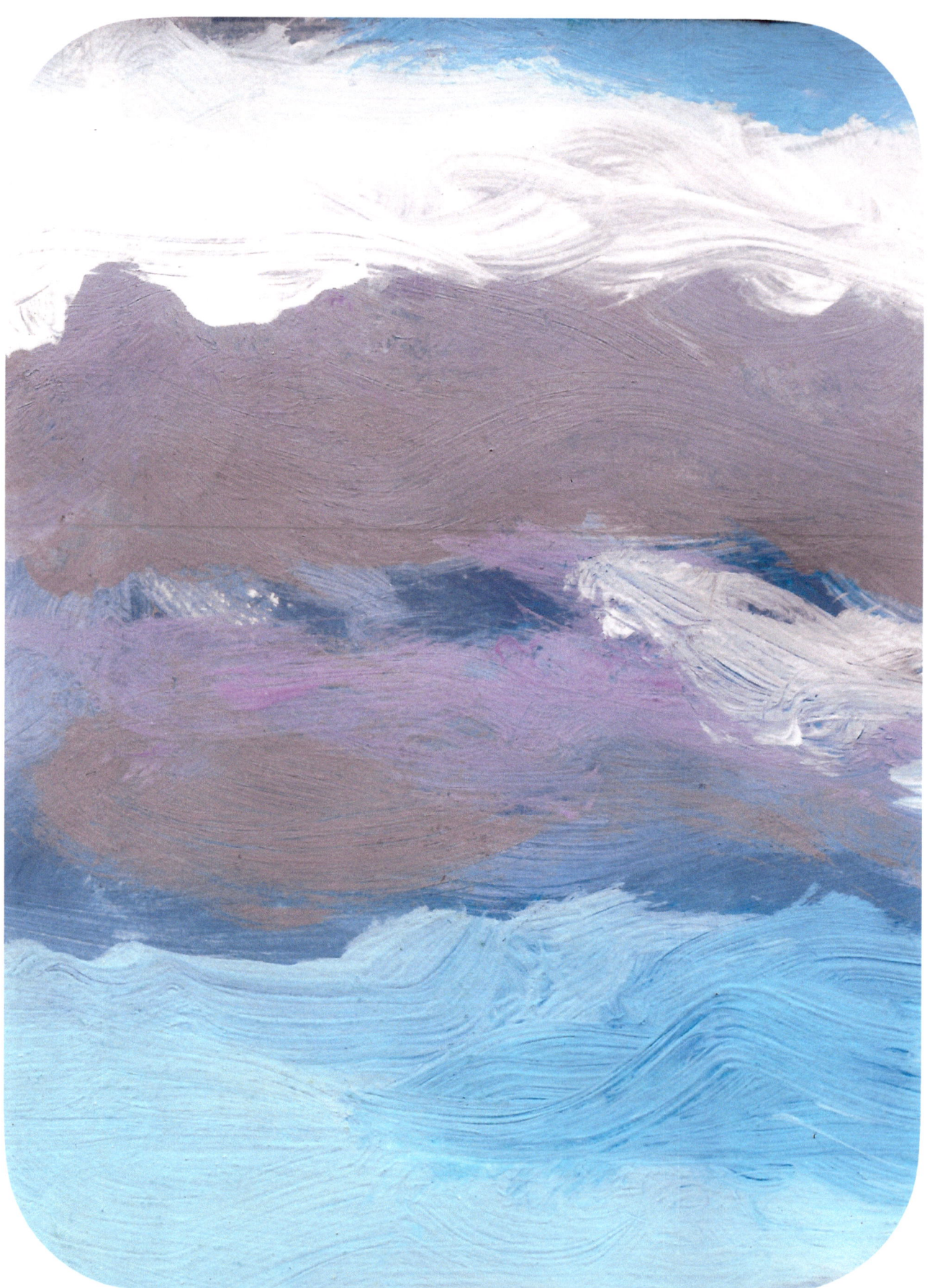

Once in a while, when the crowds get too big to handle, I start to focus on the sky above, examining the clouds and how they mimic the people on the beach. I try to remember the shapes and the colors. I find it very relaxing.

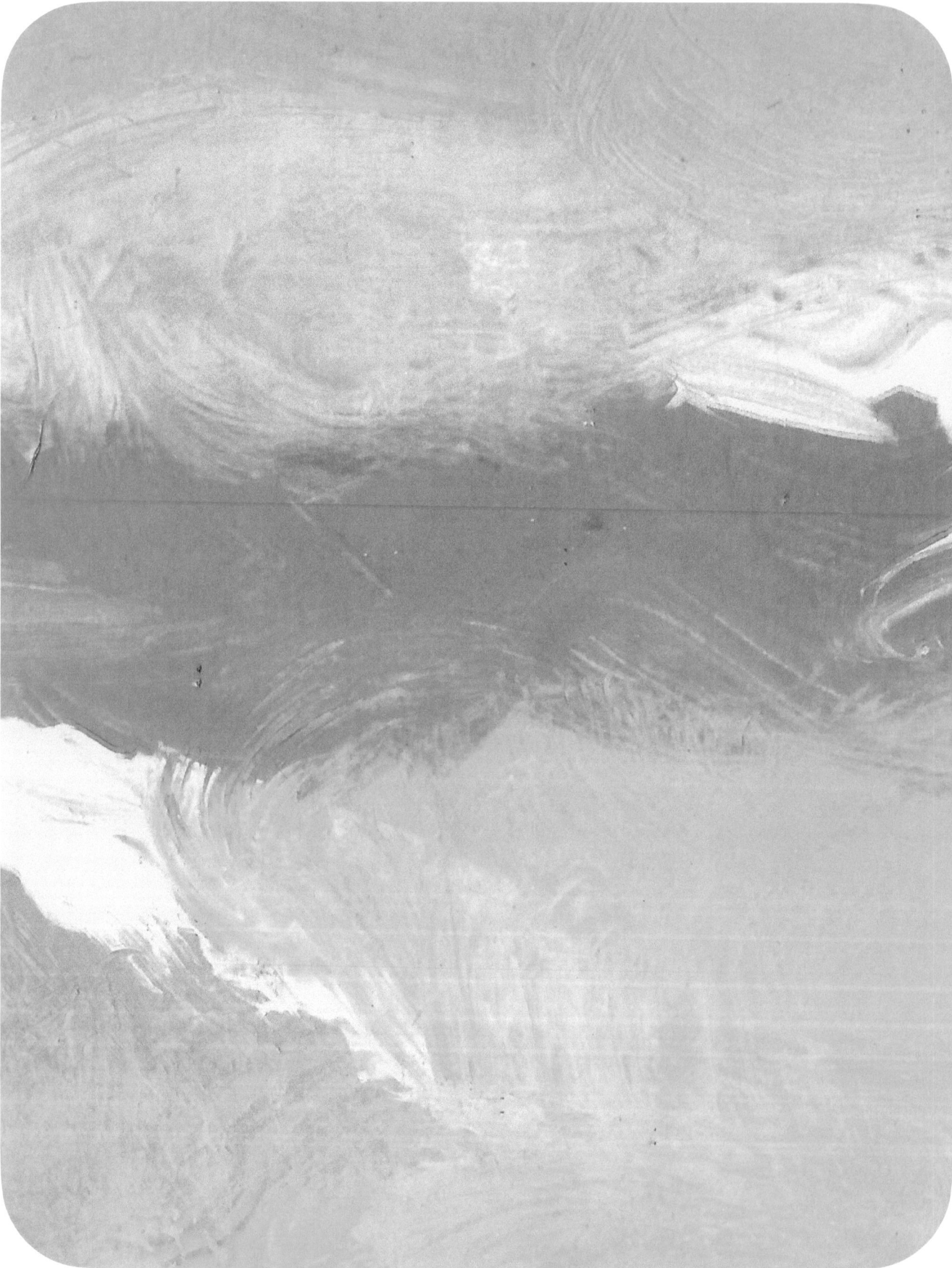

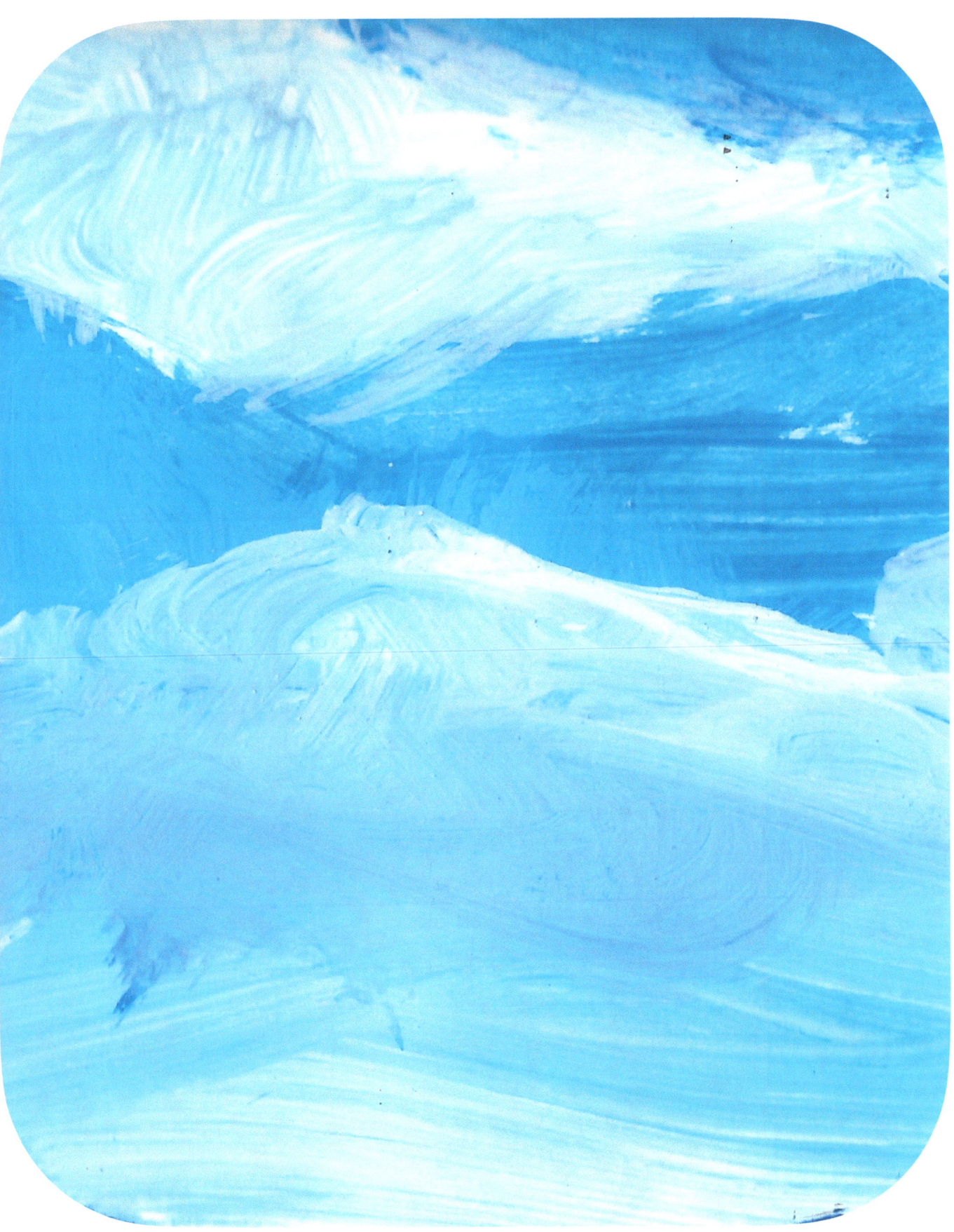

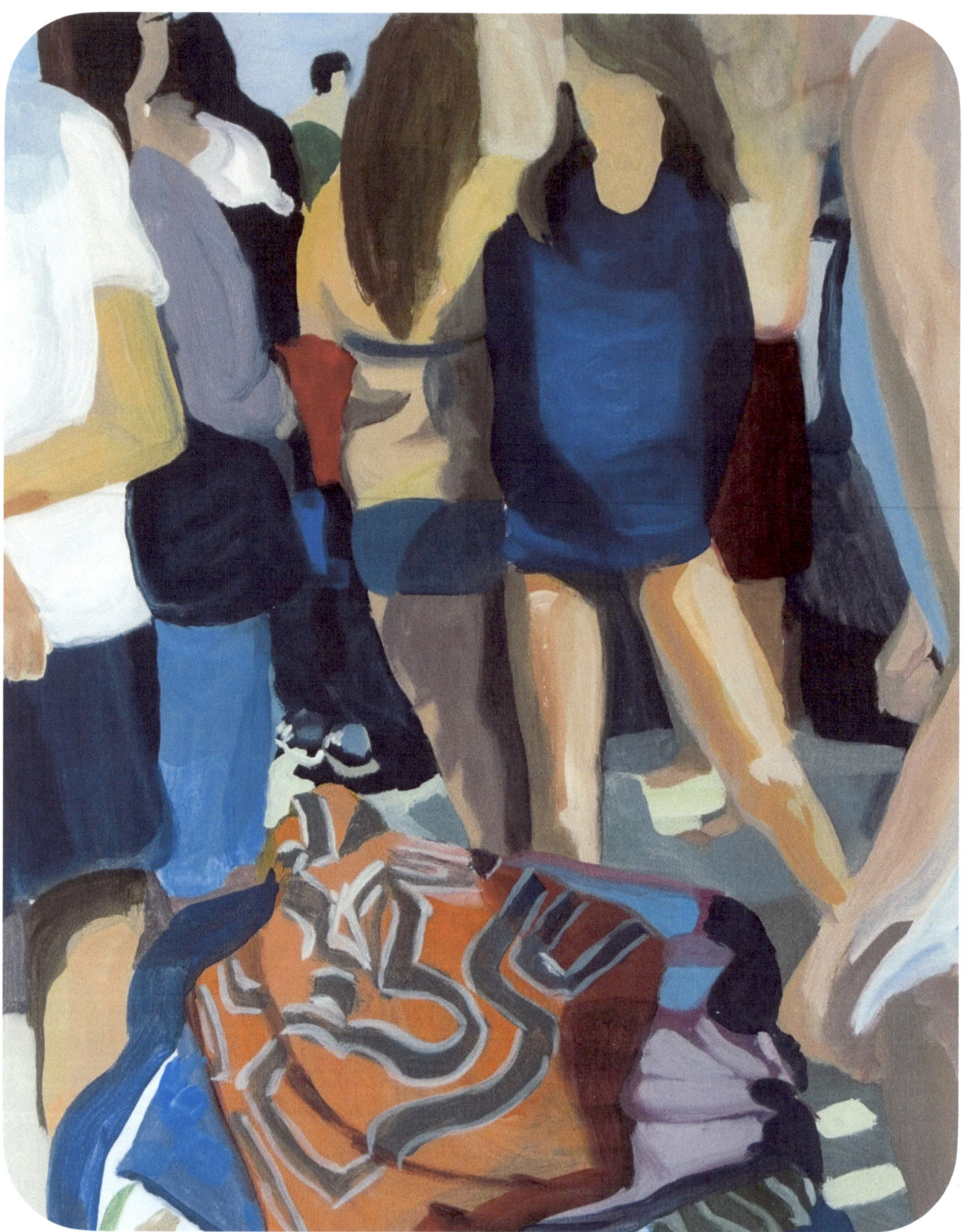

Nobody sees me when I go out on the day of the swim; I don't see them either. All I see are the shapes of the crowds. I try to stay focused for as long as I can. I draw every detail that I see.

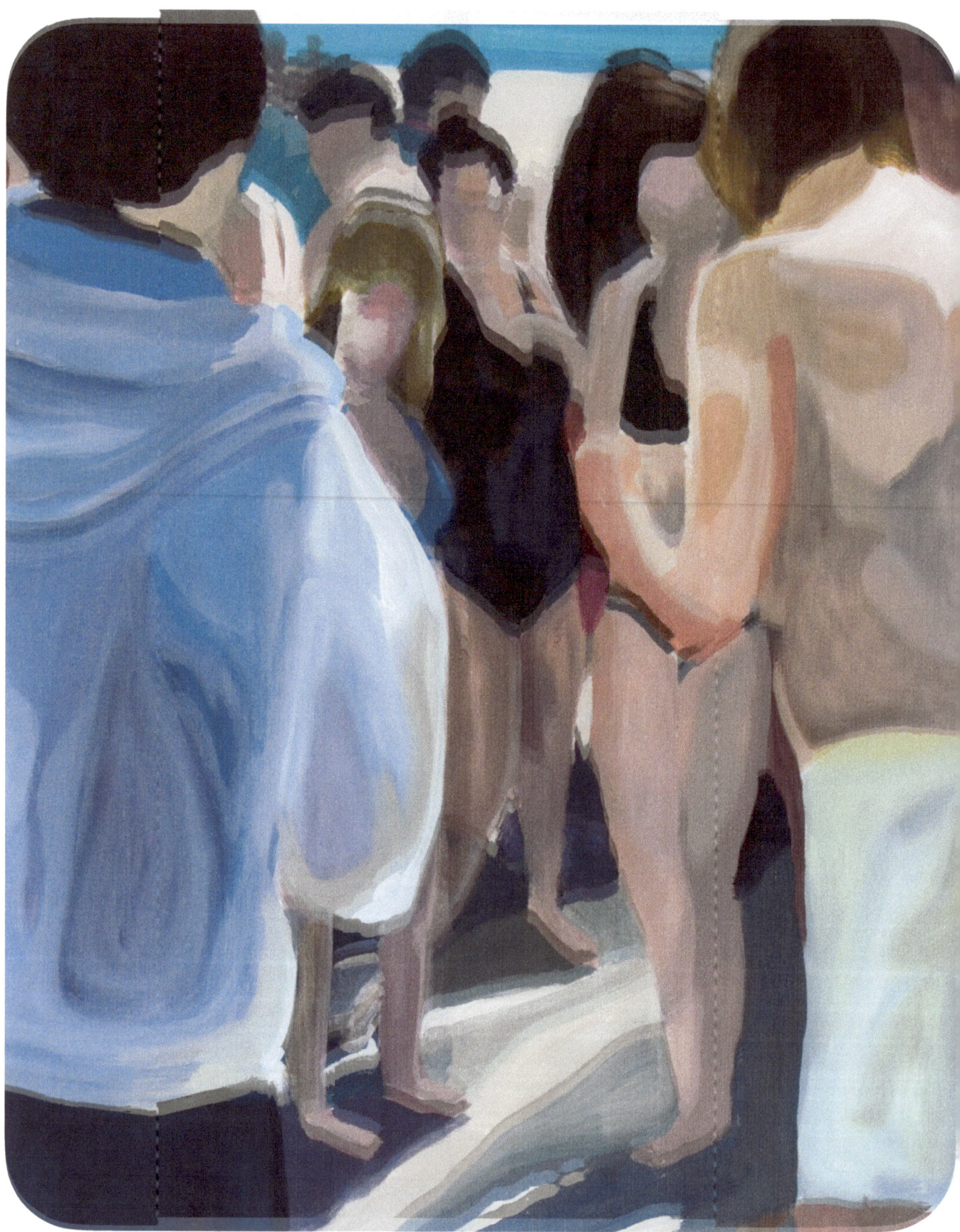

All the action happens very fast. As soon as I feel like I am doing well, the moment is over and everyone gets ready to leave.

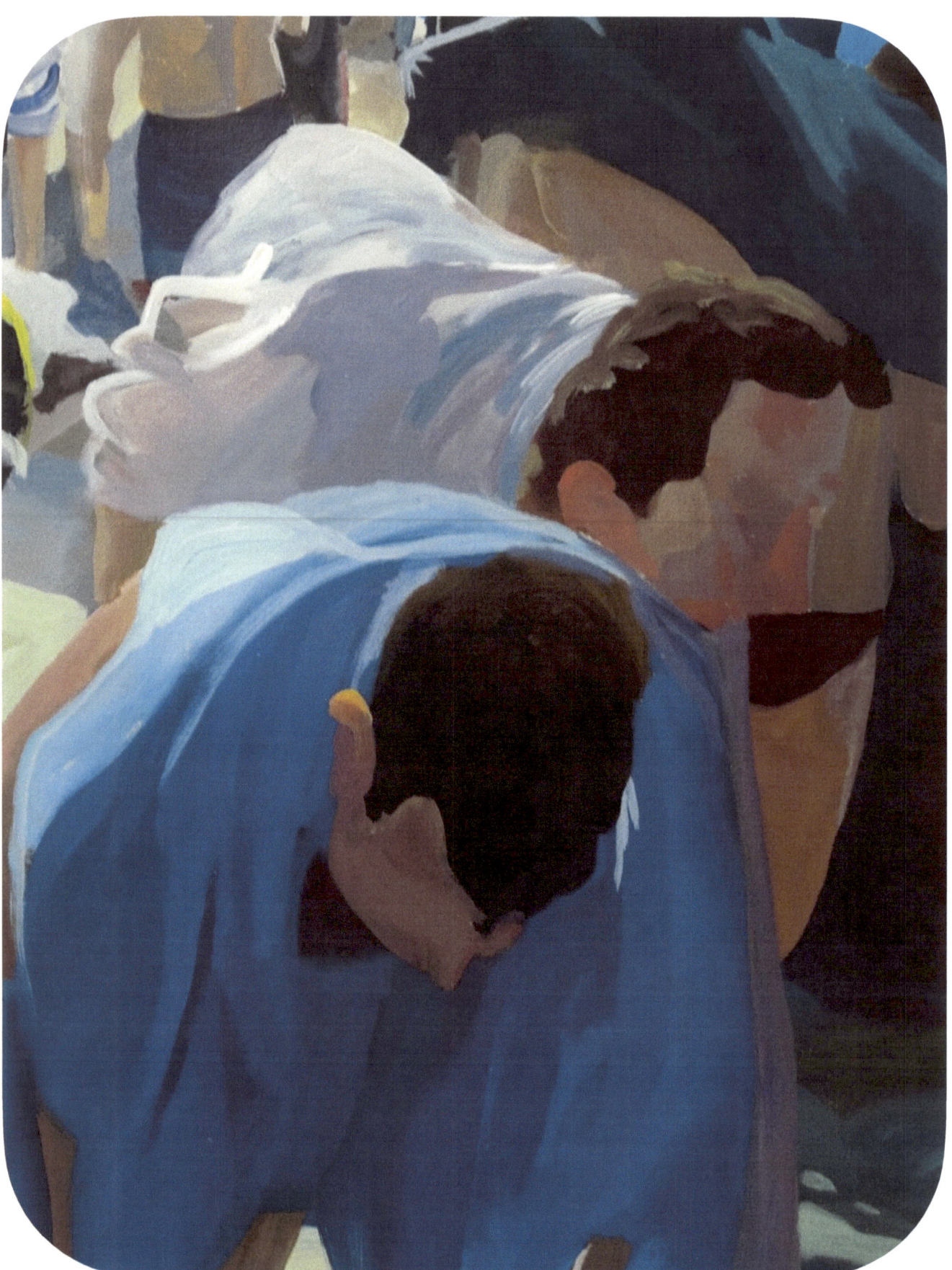

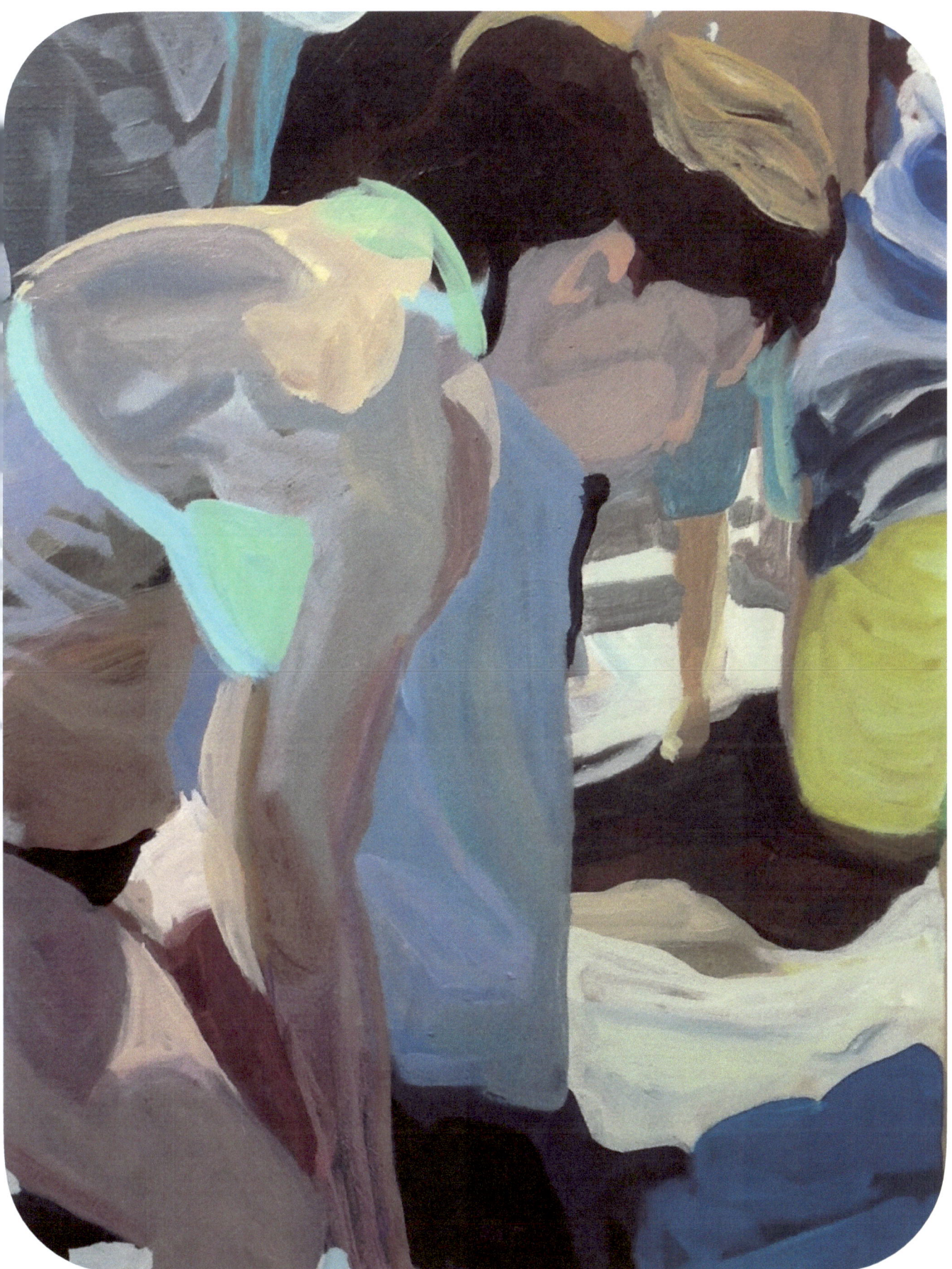

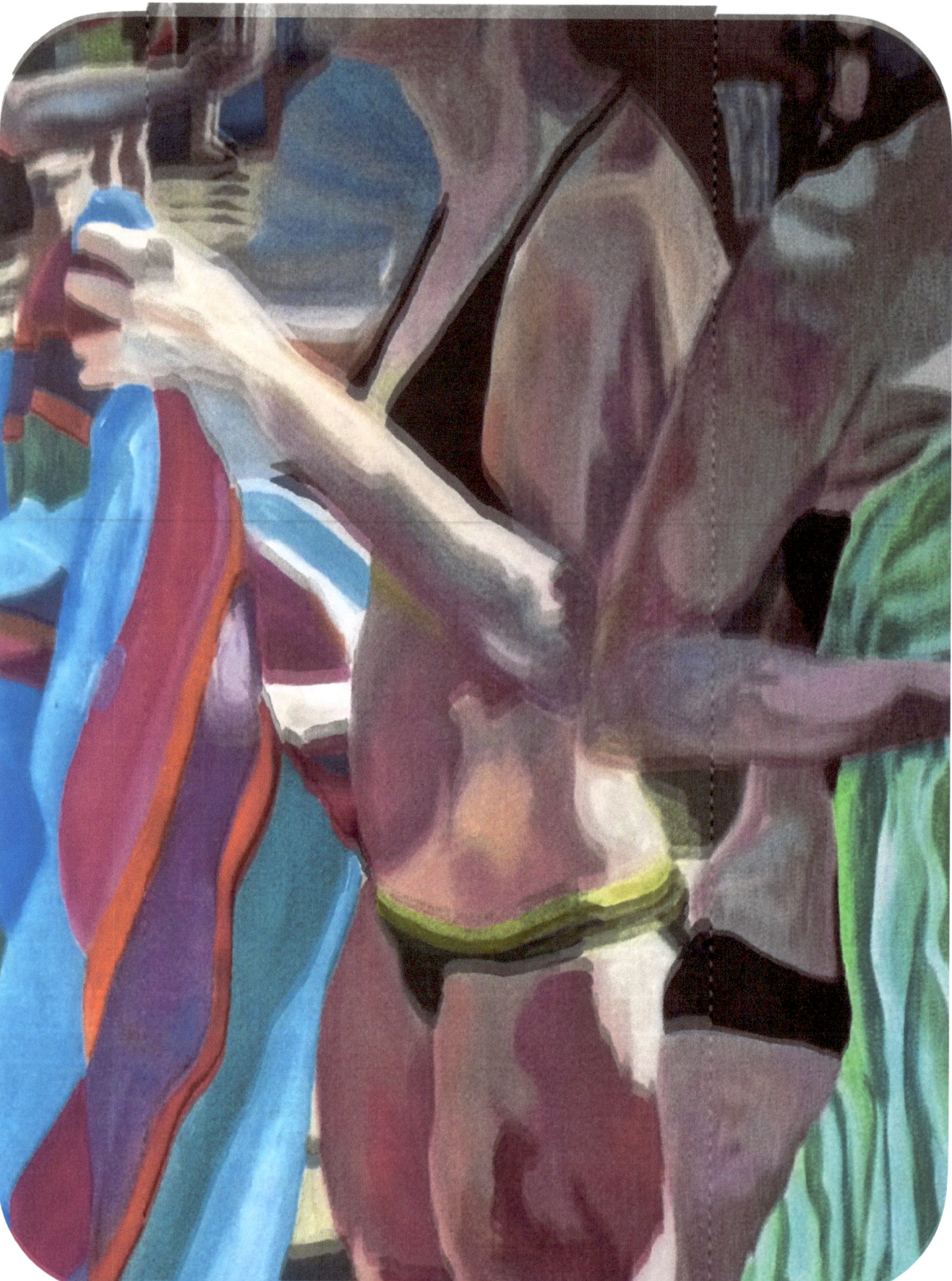

On the day of the swim, I usually stand very still and try not to make any sudden movements. I keep my sketchbook and pencil close and try very hard to capture what I see in drawings and paintings.

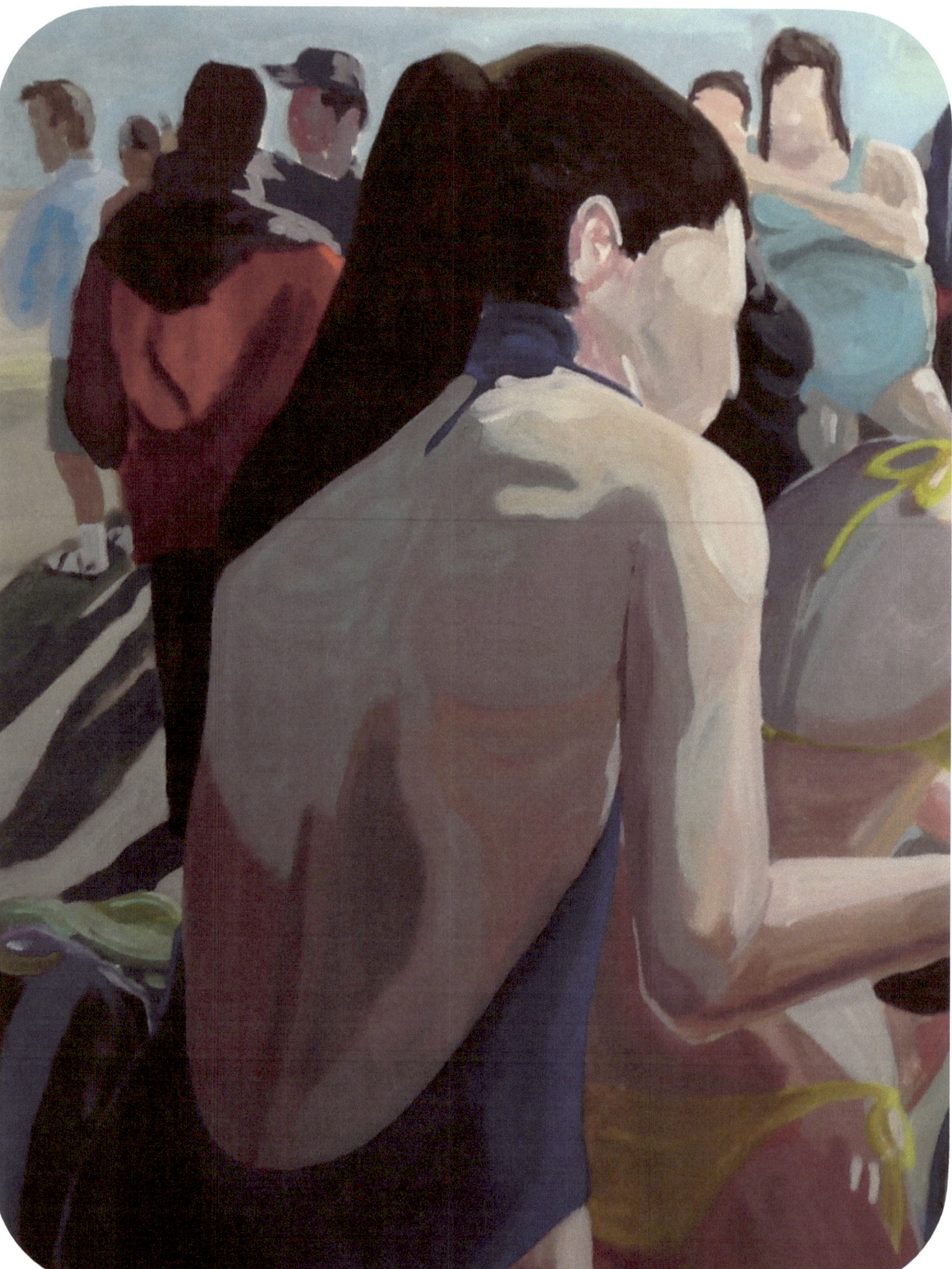

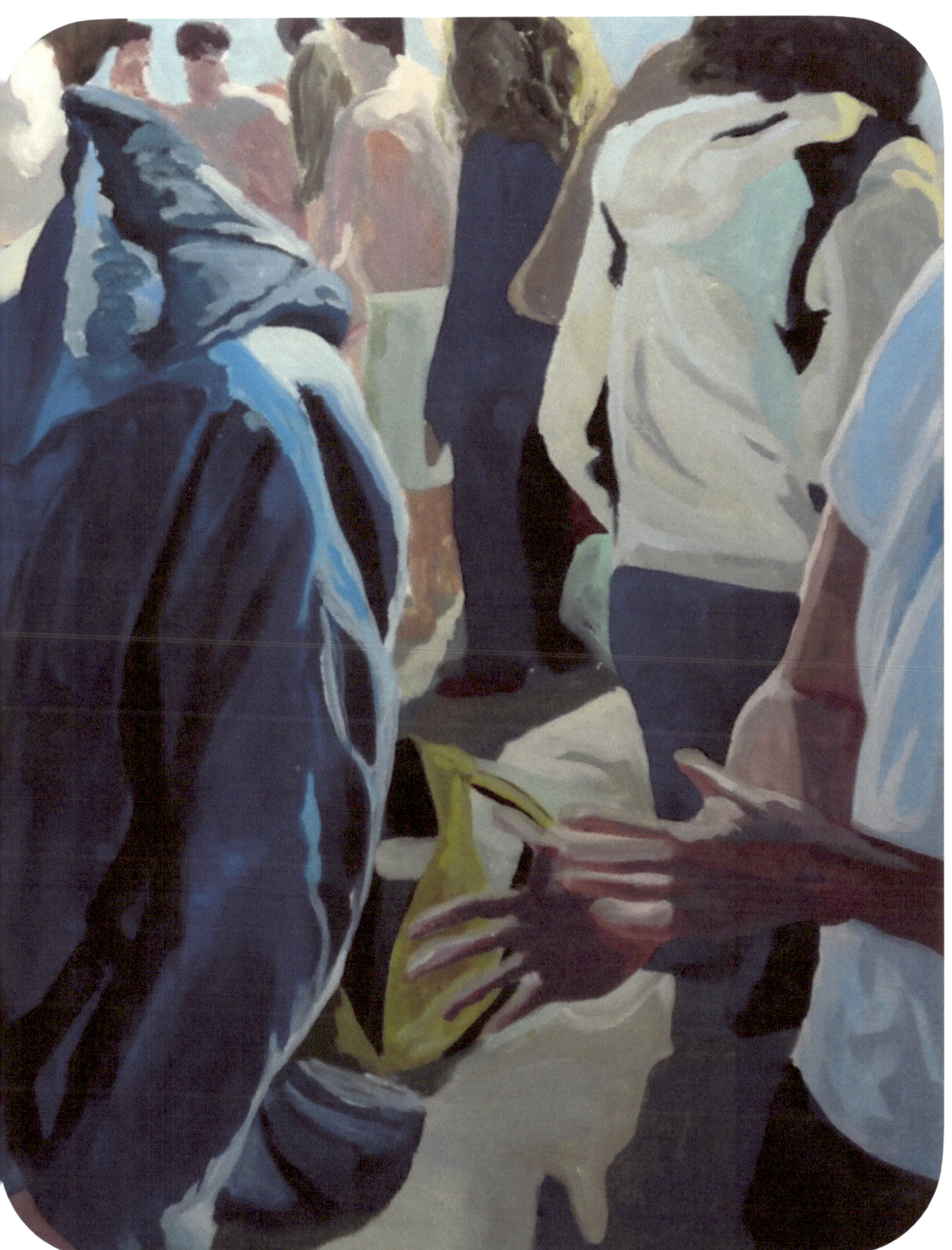

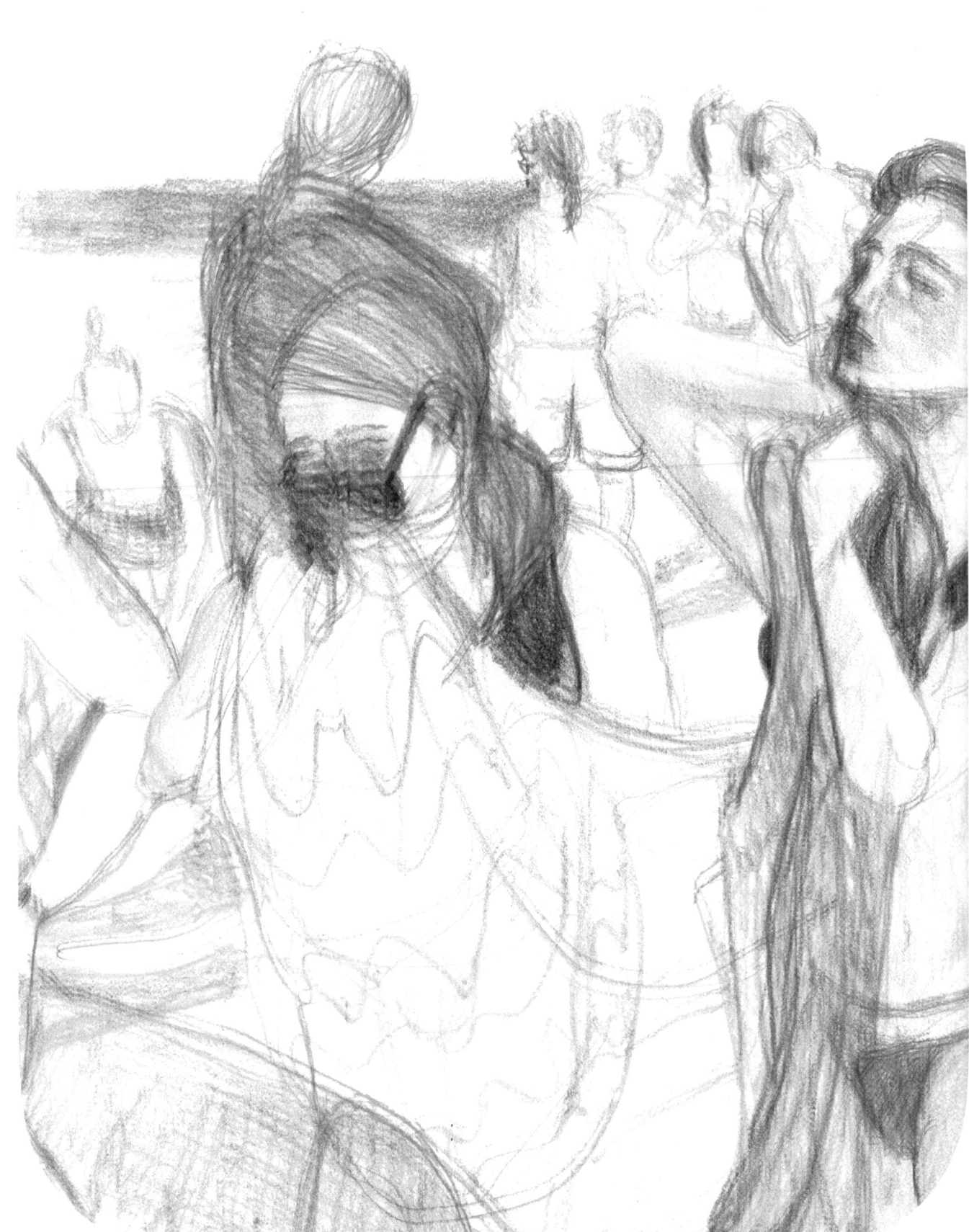

The crowd starts to thin out slowly. I can see the water. It looks cold. I don't like the cold.

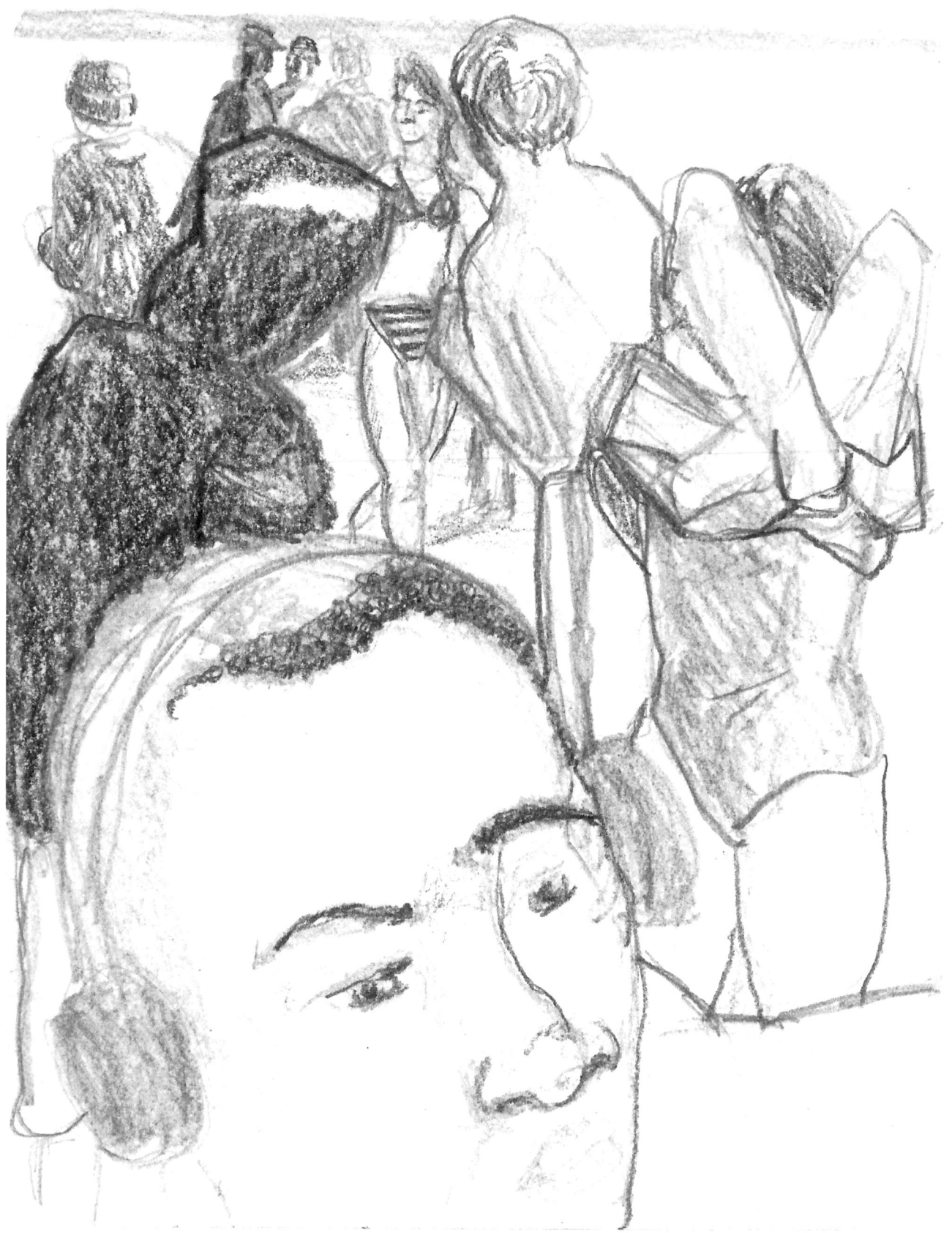

I don't like to go in the water. Maybe next year I'll jump in. I don't know.

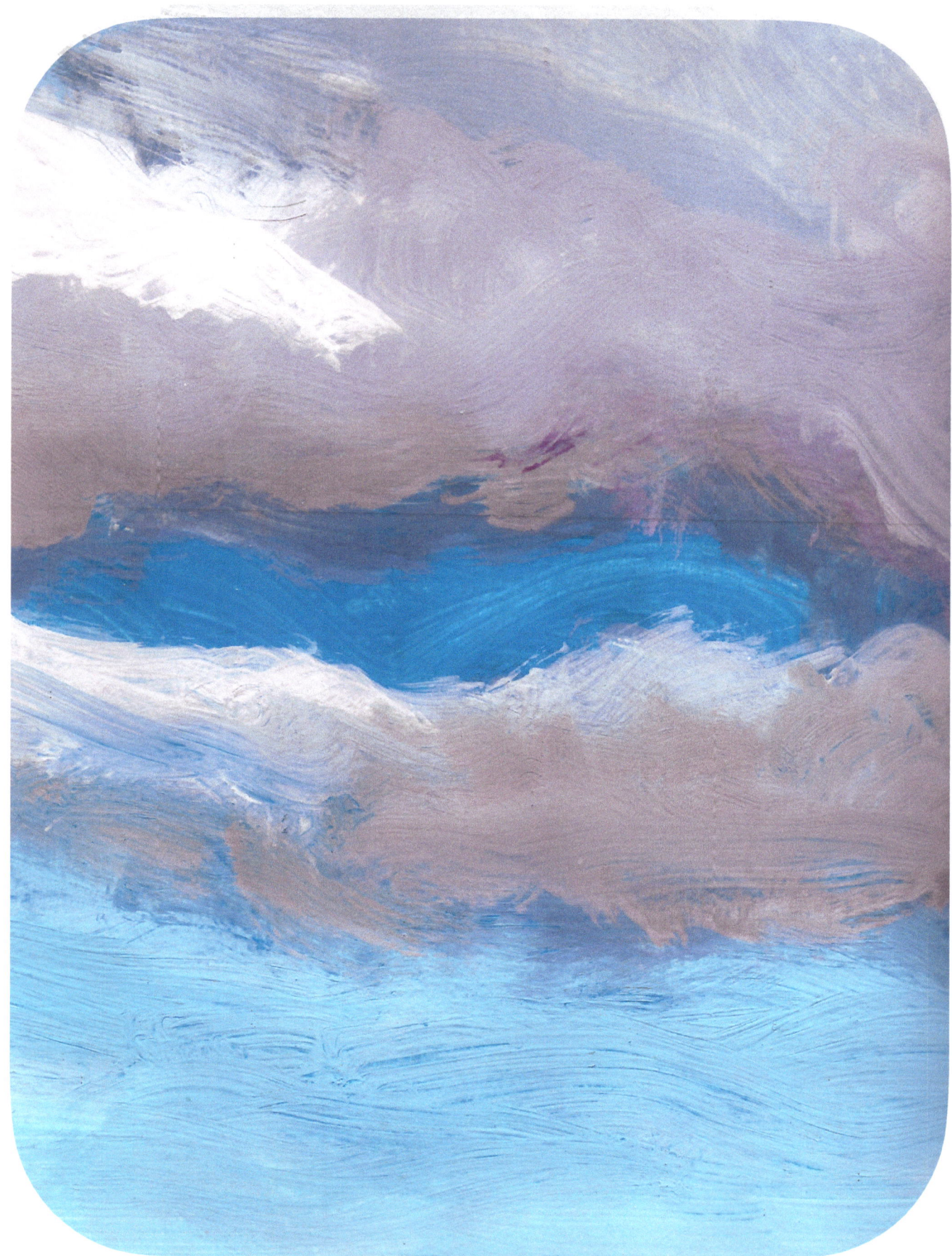

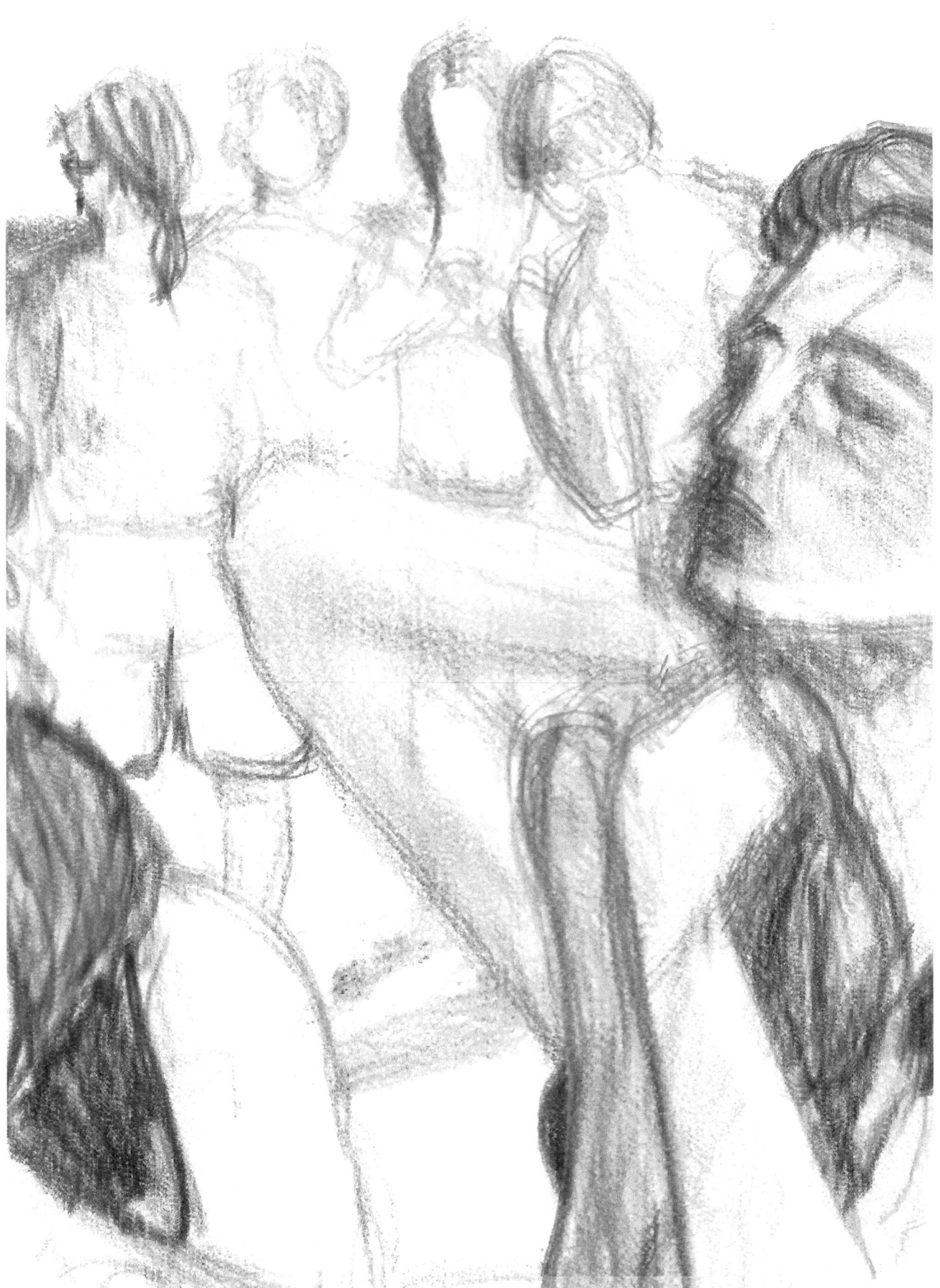

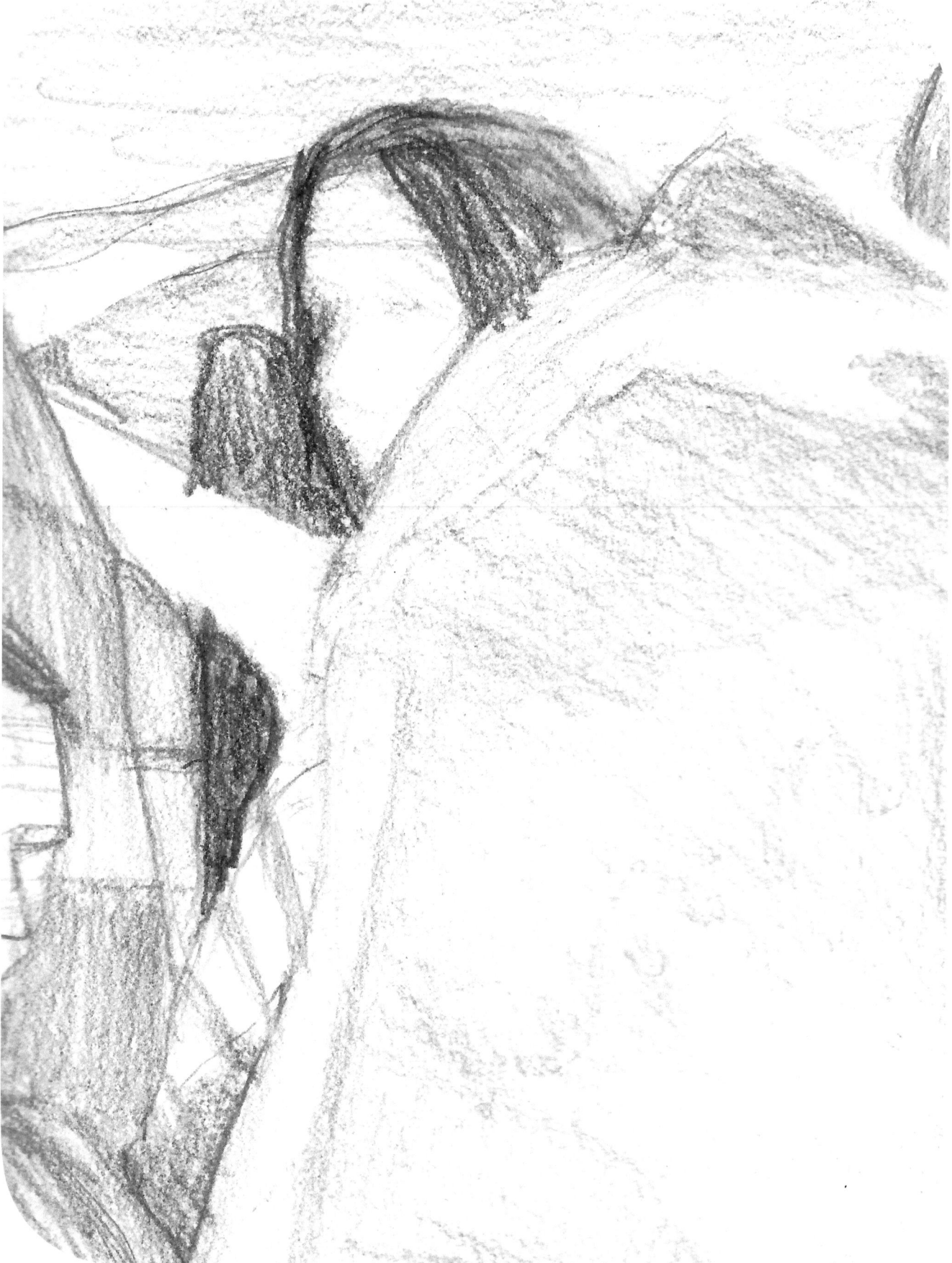

www.ingramcontent.com/pod-product-compliance
Lightning Source LLC
Chambersburg PA
CBHW051929210526
45473CB00006B/2184